LIKE A BIRD RELEASED

There's a small boat made of china
going nowhere on the mantlepiece.
Do I lie like a lounge-room lizard
or do I sing like a bird released?

~Neil and Tim Finn, *Crowded House*

LIKE A BIRD RELEASED

NAOMI THIERS

sligo creek PUBLISHING

ISBN: 979-8-9911983-8-7

Cover Photo by Chris Charles
Book and cover design by Alan Abrams

Second Printing March 19, 2025

Sligo Creek Publishing Co.
Silver Spring, MD 20901
www.sligocreekpublishing.com

For my family, past and present,
and in honor of my father, Gerald Raymond Thiers,
Dec. 1933 – Aug. 2024

CONTENTS

Song in the Dark

Song in the Dark

Will you take *all* my youth, yank out
every pearl, leaving me stunned, mouthing
a garbled message in the dark?

How many friends of my heart
are dead now, or their bold strokes dimmed
(by you) to faded things flailing in the dark?

How can my tired spirit find companions
like that again, bright sisters
to laugh me through this falling dark?

My tarnished body will never
gleam like the ingot it was, to lure someone.
No. So, am I shelved, a box in a dark

basement corner no one goes to?
No one sees two faint glows—eyes.
I'm still looking out, singing badly in the dark,

for I must make noise or be buried,
must daub on color or be taken for a dead tree.
If I walk lightly, you can't catch me, your dark

cold hand will close on nothing, stayed
one more day. I'm buttoning my striped sweater,
now, finding earrings. It's a cold evening, dark

by five, but I can walk to the park. I see
a friend there sometimes. There's that busker.
I'll clap for his harp in the early dark.

Another Morning in My 60's

Waking up every day is like
that last haul up the brutal trail to stand
at the top of Mt. Mitchell, highest peak
in the East (as I did one humid
June, sleepy then too). Disturbed
dreams swirl in the air, snake around
my limbs to pull me down.
My mind is a flat hum, muscles say No. *No.*
Nerves, firing in obscurity, still spark
with signals from REM sleep.

But as my feet drop from the bed, I feel
the trail beneath them, a well-chosen path
where I need no Sherpa, steps I could climb to rise
higher, even if morning never came.

And then, despite my tiredness,
the chill floor, ache like grit in my shoulder,
and all the old depressions—I sense
a tang in the air, a waft reminding me
of the roll and spice of spruce forest
seen from that mountaintop,
a promise:

Things may not always go as expected.

Speaking Against

I speak against safety, accommodation,
the tucking in of grief and desire—
twins we should let explore with abandon.

Let me live my last years on a wire,
under all faces of the treacherous sky,
whirl close to the fire.

The timid ones crouch in their places, strive
to avoid the eye of death or pain,
cradle their tiny rewards, then die.

I'll follow those who camp in rain,
teach a child or fall in love past 70,
if desire stakes its claim.

Let me play the horn of plenty,
as my body fades toward annihilation,
a march for the climb against gravity.

Don't give me old-people rations!
I reach for the last berry through the briars.
I speak against safety, accommodation.

The Hundred Fragile Threads

The great renunciation which old age makes in preparation
for death. . .which may be observed whenever life has been
unduly prolonged, even in old friends bound by the closest
ties of mental sympathy, who cease to make the necessary
journey or even cross the street to see one another.
              ~Proust, *Swann's Way.*

I am drawn to the airiness inside young people's eyes.
I enter and want them to teach me to dance.
I often feel above air myself,
tethered *just* enough.

I fear the hundred fragile, threads that connect
me to my past, my actions, and what-is-this-
object in my fingers? But I fear also
the breaking, the way we will each shrink to our own
private space, no matter how tightly woven
the bonds or how they gleamed--
will we cease to make the journey
even to that treasured meadow?

And I fear those whose threads are frayed
to a hair's width. They are fading,
gaunt, bones as sharp
as the razor of sadness.

The Losses

Dancing on the narrow blade of my life, I can't
help but remember when I had a wider floor
and bright partners.
    I peer into the archway of losses,

souls I thought would see me to the end,

voices I recall and would pay gold to hear again.

One ground by the boot of cancer, dead at 48,
leaving two children. One brilliant spirit
sucked into worlds of delusion.
One lost to a slow sliding away, calls
and signals unanswered until 20 miles
might be a star-verse apart.

The losses claw
at my tenderness.

The Pit

"Agua!" he said, looking up at her from the pit. The sight of a human face made him realize how thirsty he was. "Agua! Agua!"

~Larry McMurtry, *Comanche Moon*

What if you don't realize how thirsty you are—
maybe near to dying of thirst, yet
all you feel is the colorless boredom day to day—
until you see another human gazing at you,
really *seeing* you. Then the yearning,
the despair bursts loose. You understand
you're alone in a pit, mouth full of sand,
heart almost dried up. Your arms, your eyes
so weak. Can you climb out, can you
ever come back to what you were?
Will the one who sees you
reach down?

Stay with Us

With your mind that sees the apocalypse
in a teacup, traces every sidewalk crack
to the lip of an invisible pit—you belong.

Or with your hands clapped on your ears from
first light to the slow walk home, the strange
commands only you hear drowning
all else out--*alone*
in the deep center of the voice
and fire—you belong.

You belong in this carnival.

If your hands flap like frightened birds,
If you have no fingers on one hand,
If you're mute, if you're afraid to leave
your house without a talisman, if you're
blind to others' pain, if your rage
incinerates or you bore your own
mother—you belong
in this carnival.

The mouth asks, the hand takes.
These wings are from the wrong nest—
That's all of us at one time
or another, and there are sequins, light,
forgiveness, and angels on dream ladders
here—enough for you.
You belong.

Note: Italicized phrases are from Theodore Roethke's poem "The Sententious Man"

In But Not Of

The acrid taste of emotion held in, flattened.
I remember hot afternoons in our house in Pittsburgh,
my mother's depression, how it walled her off.
It's like a kind of sea, she told me.
I have known the sucking.

Some feel depression as an endless falling.
When your life is sliding down a mountain,
you can't always find a way to stop or climb,
though you yearn to go back to the start.
You close your eyes and try
to accept, to just *feel* it,
but this motion is not a dance.

Yet I can be in the sea but not pulled under.
I can swim. I was taught.
Listen to the hiss and crashing of the waves,
their song.

To My Pain

You have taken my song, my sturdiness, my sass,
left me with ashes and dread.
You have taken my lightness, my laughter,
my bowl of happiness,
left me with only grit and clenching teeth.
Left me waking each morning, thinking
how bad will it be today,
how bad will it hurt?
Will I be able to find myself,
feel the pulse of me beating
within tangled strands of pain?

But I will take it back
I will take it all back.
I rise up, demand returned to me
my song, my serenity, my sapphire,
my joy, my whirl, my willingness,
my fist in the face of fear.
Hope rises in me,
like a spear, like fireworks,
like a midsummer morning,
like a deer leaping a high fence
returning to wildness--
like fireweed,
ironweed,
jewelweed.

Go Into It

When you open yourself to the emotion besieging you,
step out of your protection and *into* it,
feel it billow around you, surge against your body—
especially grief; when you fully conjure back
Patty's face, the wispy bangs and smile that healed you
over and over, or remember what your skin felt like
when you and your husband loved each other and you
heard promise in the wren's singing that spring
(then picture them as they are now: Patty just bones,
your ex holed up in his crumbling house). . .
That is to say, when you let your heart break open
and walk among the pieces, you will still know pain,
but not from inside a dark box. The world will
open itself to you, layer after layer, revealing
its power, its breadth, and the possibilities still
buried like seeds in your damaged life.

Lower the bridge, unbar the iron door,
let air slap you in the face.

This Morning

I woke to that fierce beauty of the earth
that pierces—a crow's ragged call
tearing a sky of wild blue.

That *caw-caw!*, that limitless blue--
and I was back on Puget Sound, waking
in a fresh morning in my grandparents'
cabin, running barefoot onto the deck;
spread before me, the lapping Sound,
in the distance, the mad Pacific.

The beach was rocks, sharp shells,
squirts from geoduck clams; the sea's
coldness stole your breath, but I ran
every chance I could to walk its shore,
to daydream, imagine sailing in a miniature
boat toward that vast ocean,

drifting under a moon.
Lying on a patch of sand, I'd look up
and pretend I could rise through the thin
trees and step into the sky, into—or *yes,*
away from—what I could already
perceive life would be:
the ache of beauty.

Enough Light to See By

To care for a creature, whether human or beast.
To nurture back to life, inch by inch, any shattered
being that's more
than a shadow,
to stake our love
where agony is felt.

When you were in that hospital for weeks, I dreamed
I tended a wounded wolf with a human face.
Day after day, I rolled next to it, warmed it,
rested my cheek against its pulse of anguish.

Slow as a century building, something
whispers fiercely at the creature's
ear. Hope stirs, an eye gleams. Oh—
to watch as muscles wake, as
the loved one moves, turns!

As if when a healed animal rises,
its limbs, its very cells shifting
against each other make
sparks shoot up and—
with breath—
a flame.

After

After the steamy rush of grief into our cavern,
after we held still under the weight of it or moved rotely,
barely seeing or hearing, after we surfaced—

       buildings that had stood, that we'd
seen before anguish
trickled, scalded across that year

still stood, bland and stolid,

never even shaken.

Summer, 2023

In that summer of killing heat,
the crape myrtles made me the saddest,
their massive blooms so hot-pink it hurt,
flowering like fireworks, giving their all
in a last spasm of brilliance.
Heavy branches and flower clusters bent
nearly to the ground, as if they knew
it was nearing their final season--
the resilient earth and air that feeds us
now exhausted and on fire.

Remember us, their spilling clusters
seemed to say, *remember color, lushness,*
this earth as it was.

20 Years Together

Your wide back is a boulder
I press into, my touch a pale moss
lightly coating its surface.
There's no wildfire here anymore, no
flints of bodies shooting sparks,
but there is still heat
and a frightening solidity:
This rock will stand.
This life will cling.

Riding a Chipmunk

How could the ancients have imagined the world
sits on the back of a giant turtle?
Wouldn't we feel only steadiness and plod
as—attached to a solid crust—
we rocked methodically
toward death?

For my money, moving through life
doesn't feel like that. It swirls,
it hurts, our softness forcibly exposed.
It's the blur of crack-the-whip, then
a tense huddle in a shadowy forest.
We dart past experiences—or they
past us—and glimpse only a shimmer.
A thousand days dissolve into fog.

We look delicate, velvety, but our minds
are crude and in the end we fixate
on the scents we need for survival.

Joy, that quick rush, we skitter with it,
hearts pounding; we leap, we feel
the fresh nip of March, the dancing urge--then
a hawk shadow passes, fear yanks
and suddenly we're back
in the black tunnel
of a hollow log.

LOOK HOW FAR THE LIGHT CAME

*Each poem in this section is a Golden Shovel, a form
created by Terrance Hayes that uses one line of another
poem (by a different poet) as its basis.*

*Each of these Golden Shovels is based on a lyric by
singer/songwriter Bruce Cockburn.*

Morning, Four Mile Run Creek

The creek fingers her jewels, flirting with the sun
before 7:00 for the first time this spring. Ducks ruffle up,
the black rat snake as long as a child looks
out from it's cracked-asphalt cave, says *OK*
maybe I don't hate the world.
A fox nestles in her den, a raccoon survives
in six square blocks with five dumpsters to sneak into.
Deer eat green shoots, having made it thru another
winter. The creek sings unaware into the day.

From Bruce Cockburn song "Wondering Where the
Lions Are": *Sun's up, looks OK. The world survives into another*
day.

The Northern Lights

stunned me. I wasn't the same after
I stood by a lake, saw white plumes rain
and flare like ghost headlights down an empty street,
the sky throbbing with pulses of green light,
whorls of white, sudden vanishings, flows.
An unseen finger scribbling on the night, like
some god signing its bright name, bleeding
light like ink.
                              This vision I can
never unsee, even 30 years past, though I just
saw it once, light that shattered all rules—foretaste
of the limitless afterlife? A swirling assault
on a calm sky. For an hour, on
that shore, we watched. It was humid,
flies bit, but we stared 'til the last flare died.
                              Then wind
caressed the lake and we slept, not the same after.

From Bruce Cockburn song "After the Rain": *After the rain in the streets light flows like blood. I can just taste salt on the humid wind.*

Moods

I twirl high, bright as a ceili sometimes
then slink, a matted dog, down the
path to a paupers' field, the pitted road
that ends among wide flat stones.   Morning leads
me back to a meadow, singing through
wildflowers. Then—why?—
   something tilts, a dark
burr of fear, a black stalk replaces
the blossom in my hand.
     Sometimes
the changes blow hour by hour: blaze, darkness
drench, drought, St. Elmo's fire. What is
this curse I walk with—and what is your

patience to walk with me through it, matchless friend?

From Bruce Cockburn song "Pacing the Cage:" *Sometimes
the road leads through dark places. Sometimes the darkness is your
friend.*

In Secret

I'm an old woman. My face shows no mystery.
Who would know I once took her clothes off as the
moon
kept its white face indifferent, rising over
the mountain? Or talked with a man outside a junkyard,
trying to understand someone from a land where
the invisible, the dreamed, seems most real? Or
                        walked in snow
for a blissful day, composing in my head? My joy lies
in memories no one cares about, bright
talismans from when I gleamed.   If I set
my face like a vault, if I'm silent, it's so my heart
won't spill its jewels into the air, the fuel to
light my final days. In secret, I burn.

From Bruce Cockburn's song "Mystery": *Moon over
junkyard where the snow lies bright sets my heart to burn.*

Muse Call

I build things out of music and my imagination.
Sound architectural tools I use.
My boss is the muse. –
      ~Laura Nyro, "Serious Playground"

The fluid dances are no longer centered.
My femur refuses to play nice along
its patella. My flirtation with the earth—silenced.

Who threw my coloratura down a well? Done counting
measures 'til its high C thrusts, twirls on
surprised ears. Through drier cords—nothing.

As I turn away—a call.   I
can't leave this serious playground. I saw you

and, preposterously, saw myself standing

on the shoulders of mutilated giants on
the widest island in the
center of the sea.

From Bruce Cockburn song "Creation Dream": *Centered*
on silence, counting on nothing, I saw you standing on the sea.

Can't Help It

I can't help it: tonight, random grim
fears flood my head. My son and I have been travelers,
through years of eking out, stacking pennies, movers in
my old heap to cousins' couches. A streaky dawn,
from a Greyhound chugging down Rt. 96, skies
chopped by smokestacks, dark halls in apartments they
never tend–these things we've seen.
But always had clothes, Christmas, PO box for the
checks. Tyler finds clovers, bugs—small beauties.

This year checked all the boxes. August makes
three family dead and one car.
We'll stay in Lansing, forget them,
maybe. My fears will dry up, and his nightcries.
I'll pretend I'm going on a long ride--but in my head. Inside.

From Bruce Cockburn song "Grim Travelers": *Grim
travelers in dawn skies. They see the beauty, makes them cry inside.*

The Year It Found Me

How many glowing roads beckoned that year—a sky full.
My life shone. I didn't know what anything was made of,
only knew I'd never be ordinary, a promise rippling
inside. I strode to my first job, then . . . panic, a cliff,

freefall--as if I stood paralyzed over air. Shame and
obsession overtook me, all roads led to a chasm.

I didn't know this was my heritage finding me, that
my mother, like hers, at the same age lost her shine,
saw her bright roads fill with fear, rituals like
those I clung to all that kept her safe. I know the signs
now of those who took this journey, see on
their faces souvenirs of darkness, a place in their
eyes always on guard, I greet
      their quiet flames along the road.

From Bruce Cockburn song "Northern Lights": *A sky
full of rippling cliffs and chasms that shine like signs on the road [to
heaven]*.

STUBBORN BLOOD

Dreaming of Grandma Sue

Through night tunnels, you come to me,
ancient, loved woman--your wry, lipsticked smile,
your spit in the face of arthritis.

Sometimes you're in a shawl, lifting a Christmas bottle
of Bailey's Irish Cream, as in that photo,
sometimes you're leaning against Papa in your green suit.

Happiness—I will take it, your face seems to say.
I'm getting old myself now. Many nights,
feeling the aches, I mold your heating pad

around my limbs as if wrapping your sharp warmth
around a swelling sadness. I hear your laugh,
peppery, catching, a little cruel,

as I roll into another day.

Charley Sue at 18

-- for my grandmother, Charley Sue Cassidy

Charley Sue, last loved child
of a solid—but bit of a trickster—bricklayer,
had a wit and spirit my grandfather saw
at 50 feet as he walked down a staircase
she was stepping up with fresh-bobbed hair,
in 1922 at Puget Sound College.
Sue was 5' 2", bright-eyed, narrow faced,

a sharp tongue when needed, but mostly
she was joie de vivre and shaking the cage.
Sue drew the luck she needed to pull free
of Durant, Oklahoma. The morning after
she strode across her high school stage,
she pierced her ears and applied to colleges
out West, following her sister *ad astra*.

How sad that later the pierced ears,
the sparkly blue studs, would come to remind Sue
of her in-laws scorn, of the letter she found
on his desk: "Son, please don't marry that woman."
His aunts, on wedding day, asked her to remove
her church-offending earrings. Her chance
to be loved by that family was lost in that moment:

"You're lucky I won't wear a ring in my nose!"
For when charm couldn't win the love of another,
Sue built a high brick wall—like her father.

Great Aunt Bea

White hair foaming around her face like dancing cotton,
she'd wrap thin arms around us, holding
Dinah and me snug against her rayon dresses,
at the door of the old Cassidy house in Seattle
with the wraparound porch and unkempt holly trees.
Her southern accent, rich as visible sound--
"My little MA-A-N child"—her age-spotted hand
clasped on my brother's head.

She'd no children of her own, no beauty, no schooling.
When I knew her, she had only her raspy love of life,
that Victorian with its old plumbing and panic-steep stairs,
rivers of affection to pour on the children and grandchildren
of her sister (my grandmother, family baby and favorite),
and her resourcefulness. Bea patched holes in those walls,
with cornmeal and whitewash. All the years I knew her,
she lived alone in that crumbling house, made do,
swore she wouldn't leave it 'til she died.

She was stylish when young: crisp suits,
black or purple blouses, scarlet lipstick.
She married Gordon Smith from Alabama,
short man always wearing a hat and a strange smile,
a car salesman--and the *jewelry* he gave Bea:
loops of garnets, turquoise and silver bracelets,
one brooch a replica design from King Tut's tomb,
a box with a bow after each drinking binge.

I savor that jewelry I inherited
as her namesake, and wear it--but feel
a pang, as she must have, that each gift
was to distract from what he couldn't give,
a gilded apology for his drinking, for no babies,
no house of their own. *Kind of a pity*,
Grandma Sue used to say.

But *pity* isn't a word I'd use for Bea.
Bea took what came and savored it, loved what was
there to love: Her spoiled sister, the drunk she married,
her family's Victorian, her cats, her jewels,
her great nieces and nephew, whose veins, after all,
ran with her stubborn blood.

Family Story with Questions

Newborns in a hospital nursery in 1932,
lined up in basinettes behind a viewing window,
parents pressed against the glass, looking in.
A woman in a purple bathrobe--
my Grandma Sue, age 26, my grandfather
proud beside her—gazes at her son:
round face, dark hair, big and healthy.
But she's tired out, anxious; her face doesn't show
her rising love. Is that why the strange man
in a fine overcoat who's been observing them
whispers, "Can I buy him from you?"

Can I buy him from you? As a child, this tale
never stopped shocking me. Did my grandparents
look poor? Or greedy? A nice white couple,
with a strapping baby boy during the Depression
and two well-off strangers who couldn't get pregnant.
No need to slog through agencies, forms--maybe
they had some disqualifying secret. Imagine
my grandmother's aghast stare. But....was she tempted
for a fraction of a second? (They *weren't* wealthy;
she liked money, jewelry; she wasn't that maternal.)
Of course, they edged away in horror. My family
always laughed at the story, with my uncle crowing,
"From the very first, I was special!"

From the very first, I was special became
his theme in life. He made sure everyone knew it.
So I can't help wondering: what if they *had* sold him?
Would my mother have been raised a protected only
child?
Gone to a better college, not met my father,
but had a career, some joy beyond children and home?
Would *he* have been happier as a calmer family's
miracle, no shredding doubts about his worth?

Or grown up angry at being taken from his true blood,
his life's blueprint of fighting for first place?

After My Father's Death
   --for my father, Gerald Thiers

Don't let the wound seal over too fast,
so we heal and he becomes history, portraiture.
The ragged tear of grief – let it gap
open a while, let me miss him
keenly, hear wind keen in my chest.
He will fade into the one we used to know
(his broad smile, maroon vests, how he rubbed his
palms together), into a story we tell the great-grands.

But not now.
                    Keep him *almost*
there, the loose weave of a sleeve, whisper
of horn that pulls us back
at the doorway.

Let's stand quietly,
humbly, (as Jerry
often did in company) waiting

for this man we will never see again,
never twine against or suffer through even
one more day. Keep him here by
our longing to simply sit with him,
touching his blue-veined hand,
seeing him smile at nothing.

A Wish for M. H.

I hope there are sips of beauty
in your days—cupfuls even: scarlet
flowers in the courtyard of the Home,
hummingbird flash at your window,
shimmer of someone's robe, or even
in the labyrinths your mind crawls,
memories of being a girl in China.

Beauty--wherever you can find it,
take it, Mi Fong.
Block out the reality:
your assigned metal bed,
the beige lobby. Snap your thread
to the world if you must.
Have beauty.
Resist.

Rice Bike

Some interchanges
stick—right after they steal your breath.

Get-to-know-you chat with the receptionist
in a trade association where I worked years ago,
Cathy—coarse-featured, blond, blue-
collar Baltimore accent. Both of us
new-babied-up, so lots to talk about.
I had no photo on me, but she pulled out
a laminated snap of her boy
in a studio pose with curls like bronze fusilli.
"His daddy's Black but you can't really
see it in Tony." Lilt of pleasure, even
pride in that last phrase. The phone
rang before I could sputter out,
But wouldn't you *want* to see. . .

Two days later, she described
a Sunday with her current boyfriend—"way
into Harleys"—how they went to a Swap Meet:
bikers from two counties exchanging
gear, beer, and lore. "It's awful, but
they get some old Japanese motorcycle—
they call it a Rice Bike—and take turns
beatin' on it."
                    My hackles rose
(for you *can* see the Asian in my baby),
but I said nothing, faked a deadline,
slunk to my cubicle.
                    Remembering this now,

I think of the melting pot
Pittsburgh I grew up in, the names
we bandied about with, I still
believe, little vitriol. *He's a bohunk.*
Pollack and proud.

The wop pair extraordinaire—until
our white high school was slated
 to merge with the Black one.
                    Suddenly,
fear, venom, families
leaving our leafy street.
Hearing in Homeroom about The Plan,
the screaming meetings, shit
thrown at Black houses, I just pulled
a sad, serious face. (As Cathy
would never herself raise
a hammer, I would never
raise my voice.)

America, look what we possess:
a fleet of the wildest hybrid
sweet rides on the planet,
every metal, combo, add-on, and color,
junkyard mash-up to titanium e-bikes.

Look what we do:
drag one to the center,
smash it to bits.

The Girl Who Couldn't See Her Turquoise

*within me 'tis as if the green and climbing eyesight of a cat
crawled toward my mind's poor birds.* ~Trumbell Stickney

I can't remember just where
I met the young woman with light wheat hair.
On a river path asking for directions? At a Marriott
breakfast bar in the fruit line? You know dreams.
Maybe I showed her to a stairway. I do recall,
with detail, her face—crusted
pimples at her mouth, sharp
worry-crease—but her voice was calm, even
a lilt, her step was steady.
She wore a vivid turquoise shirt,
a shout of blue into a June sky.

I could almost see it when she bent her head at times:
...*the green and climbing eyesight*—but then
that shiny ripple of terror blinked off, twisted
back into a girl's plain face.

Only when I admired her shirt and she looked up
did I see that her eyes were blasted, sad,
the grey crumbs of spent erasers.
She said, "Oh. . . it has a color?
I didn't know my shirt had a color.
I thought it was the color
of nothing."

Young, still lilting, but even
sound eyesight and turquoise near her heart
. . . *crawls toward my mind's poor birds--*
could not protect her.

Do Something

This adult male, this person on earth.
Ten billion nerve cells. Ten pints of blood.
Within him, there's awful darkness,
in the darkness a small boy.
God of humor, do something about him, OK?
    ~Wislawa Szymborska

1.
A comet of sparks, flung from an endless grinding wheel:
the essence of young men—a hot blind energy,

a fierce, mute beauty. Their man faces,
frantic new hair, bodies aching into grace—but

this power can bruise. Every woman
and many men know this. What do we

do with this rain of red sparks
on our skin, dismissed as fireworks? Yes, yes

we *know* the fear and the pain young men hide
within is the heart of this burning,

but the wheel keeps grinding.

2.
I remember helping care for my little brother
when I was 5, he 3, helping him dress.
He followed me around. I called him my robin,
threw rocks at anyone who taunted him.

I think of the boys in my apartment complex
I've watched grow from pups into almost-men,
teens with newly filled biceps or awkward elbows:
Sharif, Joey, Maneer. . . About their jaws,

still a downiness. Some hold doors for me now,
nod shyly, where once they chirped questions at me.
Others stare openly, measuring. Their friends,
kids I don't know, hang in our parking lot, smoking.

A few, people say, have joined gangs. At the
ice cream truck, tattooed tears under the eyes.
Yet there's a buoyant joy to most teen boys here.
They flash by two-on-a-bike, all teeth and laughter.

3.

It wasn't a teen boy like these--rangy, urban,
communal--who held me down
and finger-raped me in the woods
when I was 11, when I felt the acid of terror
burn into my skin. He was pale, serious.
And though his act became a horse on fire running
through the field of my life, he was well-combed,
a fortress of solitude—and, though the police
apprehended him, never
punished, never made
to answer.

4.

But I have questions. Why
could this arsonist of flesh roam the woods alone
freely after that—I, never again? Why
was the shield (boy scout hardening,
boxing lessons) only for my brothers?

5.
I'm 60 now and still live with green beckoning
of woods behind my house, young men sprawled
on my porch. Oblivious, fun, hurt-concealing
boys juggling axes in the night. I ask myself:
what is in this darkness?
Why do we cradle it?
Why is a stalking panther so afraid?
Does a predator crave more pain
or just release?

God of humor and justice,
weigh in.

Old Man as a Wall

I'm blind-ancient, blasted. What keeps my stones
leaning together, gripped by bruise-green vines?
Could these tangling vines alone stop my chipped
face from crumbling to a pile of bitter dust,
hold my scraped bits standing one next the other?
Everyone who has held me, tightly or just
out of obligation, down the years, is dead. Wind
shivs in the gaps between my cold bones.
Maybe it's simple spite, defiance
of the young that keeps me standing
(I could flatter myself and call it will,
call it fierceness.) Or maybe

it's fear--for I hear the sea always,
crave release, yet fight
being pulled into its arms and dissolved,
salt and lost memories where once my body shone.

I stand, an ancient wall of blind, dumb stones.

Burden

I've noticed her for years, my eyes
drawn to her drag down the street
as if she is my prickly burden.
A skinny woman pushing a packed cart,
worn cloth bags slung over her shoulder,
a woman closed in on herself, always
silent, alone, head down, white hair
pulled back with elastic, taped-up glasses.
As much a feature of South Arlington
as The Broiler and chicken a la brasa joints,
but mostly invisible.

A week might pass with no sighting, then
there she'd be: crone toting cart and bags.

Then one day I saw her cross George Mason
unencumbered—without cart, walking freely,
white hair and arms a-swing,
head raised. *She's healing!* I thought.
She got a room. She's in the world.

Two days later, she was at a bus stop shelter,
with cart and bags again, eyes on the pavement,
as if she'd known one day of freedom,
one day of being a person—then
again shrugged on her rancid raincoat.

At Least That

I came to the cemetery accidentally.
Meandering near a lake at town's edge,
I saw I was walking toward scattered graves –
new, old, and makeshift ones jumbled, plastic flowers
crowding many. Some had photos somehow
fused into the stone, lost smiles stilled,
or engravings telling the whimsy ("Ducky" White)
or passions of a life. Fresh roses on a stone photo
of a shy-eyed young woman. . .

Sometimes we brought flowers.
We held up placards of our young
sons and daughters, their captured faces,
as our feet pushed around, around the Plaza,
as we intoned their names, desaparecido . . .

Wandering the eclectic graves, I noticed
all the faces on the stones and all the visitors –
a laughing family yanking weeds, a quiet woman
walking head down–were Black,
and the older crumbling stones were marked
for freed slaves, blacksmiths, World War I medics.
They had claimed this grassy strip by the lake
as their place.

The Plaza del Cinco de Mayo was our place,
we stubborn, hoarse mothers. Every Thursday,
in white headscarves embroidered with our dear ones'
names and "Aparacion con Vida," we demanded
the bodies of our children
(of my Eugenia, at least that).

A curious woman out of place here,
I wandered toward the back: ancient graves,
cracked, sunken, some just the cemetery disc and a ring
of smooth white stones or even a concrete block,
but a marker, a breathing space for grief.

Maria Eugenia, if we'd only had a grave,
if they'd given me some of your bones
or the last clothes you wore,
if there were a place I could kneel and know
a part of the body I'd carried, I'd held,
was there, a witness to the weight you had
in this world. Disappeared,
you shimmer, always beyond reach,
an ache clenched inside me
everywhere I go.

I'm an outsider, a woman in comfortable shoes.
Walking among true bonds in this Black cemetery,
I remember the ocean of suffering I saw in Argentina.
Here, ringed by graves, I can still see
the tortured eyes
of the *madres*.

NOTE: In the late 1970's and early '80's in Argentina, a group of
mothers whose grown children were "disappeared" by the military
dictatorship marched weekly in the Plaza del Mayo demanding
information about or the return of their children. Few of the
desaparacidos were returned. The bodies of many were eventually
found in mass graves; others remain unaccounted for.

The Year My River Ran Backwards

When I felt pulled into some whirlpool by a wave
of white shirt, his crooked smile at my door.
When—stooped, with a doughy face you'd never
guess was half Cherokee—he brought his awkward
flattery to me, his flash of saxophone skills,
sincerity in an uncool package. When I was
inside-out, flailing in a dried-up marriage,
resident in a ditch of helplessness.
When he put his hand near mine, or
on my back but no further,
when he *saw* me.
When catalyst words were coded on postcards,
flowers left at doors, and glances the half-blind
could see. When he was the reason
I came to the group, then the reason
I stopped coming—stopped just
in time,

it was as if the river of *me* that
I walk in, the flow I never thought *not*
to follow ran backwards for three months
because I let it, because I willed it to,
because all I wanted
was water.

Release

You never see a baby pigeon,
Dad used to say. Truth is, they're half
rat, and the chicks fledge in the sewers.

A bird cursed if noticed at all,
like flying litter in an urban day,
unwanted as hotel art

    —but not
Hossein's pigeons,
Hossein's joy.

Have you seen two slim white and cinnamon
birds, wing to wing, fly a purposeful arc
around a brick apartment building,

their high-lit grace like two sentient leaves
tracing a circle through late evening sky,
dipping and skimming, still twinned

to land on a man's outstretched arm
on his white shirtsleeve? Seen his dark,
dapper face split in half by smile?

An ordinary man, a teacher in Karachi,
now a taxi driver with quiet wife and four boys
living in a two-bedroom apartment.

A place of scarred bunkbeds, bins, kids
smacking each other, but on his high balcony—
contraband in a white crate.

This orderly man breaks rules—
six people in 1,500 square feet, his sons
biking through the parking lot--but mostly

with his birds who swiftly slice
our inner-suburb sky every evening. Circle
and home circle and home. At times

they land on my balcony rail, strut and tilt
their fine chocolate heads, their feathers soft, clean,
and the little boys crowd at the rail below mine

crane their necks up and giggle *Don't tell!*
and I won't, for I love this sight, pigeon grace,
love that I *have* seen a pigeon chick held

in his toweled palm (weak, pale
as dirty ice, but its neck craning), love
to see him lift his arm in the release—

his sleight of hand,
his sip of joy.

ACKNOWLEDGMENTS

I acknowledge the following publications in which these poems first appeared:

Potomac Review: "Song in the Dark"
Fledgling Rag: "Speaking Against," "Dreaming of Grandma Sue"
Anti-Heroin Chic: "In But Not Of," "Can't Help It"
Cactus Heart: "Riding a Chipmunk"
Loch Raven Review: "This Morning," "Old Man as a Wall"
Bronze Bird: "Summer 2024"
Northern Virginia Review: "Release"
Maryland Literary Review: "The Northern Lights"
WWPH Writes: "In Secret"
Passager: "Wish for M. H."
The Power of the Feminine I (anthology): "At Least That"

AUTHOR'S BIOGRAPHY

Naomi Thiers grew up in California and Pittsburgh, but her chosen home is Washington, DC, area. Her first book of poetry *Only The Raw Hands Are Heaven* won the Washington Writers Publishing House competition. Her other books are *In Yolo County* and *She Was a Cathedral* (Finishing Line Press) and *Made of Air* (Kelsay Books). Her poetry, fiction, and essays have been published in *Virginia Quarterly Review, Passager, Poet Lore, Colorado Review, Potomac Review, Sojourners,* and many others. Her poetry has been nominated for a Pushcart Prize and featured in anthologies and on public buses in Virginia. She works as an editor and lives in Arlington, Virginia.